Medic Against Bomb

A Doctor's Poetry of War

Medic Against Bomb

A Doctor's Poetry of War

Poems by
Frederick Foote

GRAYSON BOOKS
West Hartford, Connecticut

Medic Against Bomb: A Doctor's Poetry of War
Copyright © 2014 by Frederick Foote
Published by Grayson Books
West Hartford, CT
www.graysonbooks.com
Printed in the USA

Foote, Frederick.
Medic against bomb : a doctor's poetry of war / poems
by Frederick Foote.
pages cm
ISBN 978-0-9913861-1-6

1. War poetry.   I. Title.

PS3606.O68M43 2014   811'.6
                                      QBI14-600009

ISBN: 978-0-9913861-1-6

Book & cover design by Cindy Mercier

For the members of the Military Health System
and the Veterans Health Administration, who found ways to heal

"For every thing that lives is Holy." —*William Blake*

CONTENTS

PART III: RUINS OF PEACE

PART IV: CODA

INTRODUCTION

After 29 years of "caring for those in harm's way" as a U.S. military physician, I wanted to think seriously about war, and to allow others to think along with me.

Some believe lethal warfare will last forever. But lethal war is a violation of the sacred, a taking by men of human lives that belong to God. Since God is bigger than we are, I doubt this scenario will play out forever.

I believe in fact that lethal warfare may not outlast this century. As we evolve new tools, both social and technological, for engaging in conflict, we should find less abominable ways of conducting our contests of will. What happy warriors we'll then be, free of the taint of murder that now darkens the trade.

Beyond that, I imagine soldiering will be much the same. Discipline, sacrifice, and measured pain are what strengthens a human will. And conflict, which is our path to justice, will always be the duty of those who guide the community.

Some of these poems date from the cruise of the hospital ship Comfort (T-AH-20) to the 2003 invasion of Iraq, where we saw mostly Iraqi patients Medevaced to the ship. Other poems emerged from the care of sick and wounded American Warriors (Soldiers, Sailors, Airmen, "Coasties", and Marines) and their families. All are as true as I can make them.

The stories of mourning are of course also true. Mourning is the only universal product of our current system of war. As the ronin Kambei says in "Seven Samurai," soldiers always lose.

I have loved and honored them from my boyhood and always will.

Frederick Foote
Captain, Medical Corps, USN (Ret.)

CONTACT

You Gave the Iraqis Their Scarves
for Doctor Pat McKay

When limbs are lost
who stops to think
of clothing thrown away?
Who knows the shame
of sheltered girls
on sudden public display?

And so within
the non-combatants' ward
they neither prayed
nor shrank from pork
but showed their skin
with vacant-eyed sangfroid
knowing that since
the world had burned alive
it didn't matter.

You came out of the O.R.
night after night
and wrote your orders
just as the men would do
but then, instead
of clumping off to bed
or getting drunk
on bootleg DVD's

You'd find a place
no one could observe
bring out an ancient
Singer sewing machine
and squares of silk
left over from a quilt
the nurses made
to celebrate our work

And there each night
like the breath of a word

You'd sew, quietly sew
as the ocean weaves a reef
together after a storm
binding polyps
and tiny fish
bringing grass
back together with stone
with overflowing
largesse of patience

The day you brought the scarves down
they pressed your hands
and those not lamed
tied scarves around the heads
of friends who couldn't move
        (silk to die for
        new to those
        dust-colored homes
        only the F-18s
        had deemed worth bombing)
those who thought
they could no longer weep
wept to feel the touch
of simple cloth

And they were once again sacred women.

The Hurt Fedayeen

We shot him through the chest, and now we're saving his life;
it seems absurd, but that's what Americans do—
blow a place apart, then put it together again,
pretending it's good as new.

We won't recall his face, he's just a pin in the map
on which, day after day, the war's reborn—
there's always a clean glass eye, a limb neat from the rack,
a fresh martyr to mourn,

while past the sandbagged door, there on the camera set
where CNN packs up the network news,
the maimed world lurches by, calling out for bread,
unwilling to die of wounds.

Local News

Enter the E.R. after the choppers leave;
you'll see, without requiring to be told,
in forty-two beds that writhe or fight to breathe
the new Iraq that's winnowing out the old.
The girls with legs blown off were brought from Qut;
the man from Nasiriyah's lost his sight—
I only know because I dressed their wounds;
they're like familiar lamps against a night.
With each charged day, each unrelenting sun,
a land of ruin dawns irreparably—
My friend, what have we raised, what have we done?
This never was a world we wanted to see.

Nursing the Iraqis

Here's how I learned their tongue: *Sadeek! Sagheer*
amaliyaa (small operation) —he goggled at me—
La alam! La alam! (No pain) took the edge off the fear—
we had no translators— infallible DoD.
That came from a Berlitz book, a nightly task,
after the wounds, the unrelenting burns had had their run...
We must have seemed half- mad. Doctors chanting on rounds,
nurses warbling, corpsmen speaking tongues,
never since Babel such overflow of sound.
One phrase—*Salaam Alaykum*— stilled every alarm:
it showed in the face, the terror yanked like a mask—
No one who knew God's name could mean them harm.

Doctors nursing wounded soldiers
they learned language as well as they could to make
patients feel better.

Soldiers' Chorus

You've heard of crimson rivers where the power of dark resides—
Wrap your arms around me, I'm taking you for a ride.
Down in Brimstone Valley lives a spider with feet of brass—
We'll hump him home to party, then the devil may take the last.

A-K's are slick as ever, RPG competes with TOW,
And those on third deployments understood it long ago.
At dusk in hot Ramadi, land of killing zones and tombs,
The gunners speak their purpose while the tracer splits the gloom.

Red dust goes up your nose, the heat's one-twenty in the shade,
The soldier in the hatch takes pointed rounds the rest evade.
A thunk on body armor lets you know you're living still—
The medics mind their business— nine are maimed for each one killed.

The troops have got a wager, who will drop and who'll survive—
A promise that transparent seems certain to be a lie.
It shines like resurrection, till it turns to shock and shame:
Such a golden opportunity to romp awhile with pain.

Night Mission

Over the pitching seas,
I watch before the dawn
the helos crouching down,
the files of tense Marines.
They're going behind the lines,
moving from ship to land;
Medical's overmanned:
this time I'm left behind.

Staggering under loads,
they face the Frogs and board,
stolid against the shore,
like Marius' Mules of Rome.
A wave from one I know
sitting amid his men—
he says he's here to defend
his daughter who just was born.

I need to make you hear
rackets of shots and bombs—
witness the outer calm—
picture the inner fear—
to show you the reason why
I and my kind have sworn
to stand in the fire for
such valiant, threatened lives.

Darkness beyond the bridge,
distant bolts of light—
they're taking rounds tonight,
we're bringing the wounded in.
Remembrance torn from above
murmurs a brace of names—
may I, in the hour of flame,
reveal a similar love.

Ahmed the Soldier

Just like someone opened up a pop can —the skull's lid free—
still tied into his truck burned black by the F.A.E.—
we saw in awe— but what should least have survived that wreck—
the picture of wife and baby girls— is what I'll never forget.

Mujahadeen

Remnants of the files of al-Kunar
ascend in broken lines.

The rest have died like the men they were,
souls of bright metal.

Our feet have proved the righteousness of peaks:
our journey to rest is fighting.

Cries of Heaven beyond these hills
probe our flesh like knives.

My two noble sons
will know the end of my climb.

Space Travel

for Cassandra Spears, R.N.

Twice a day it welled up, on the Iraqi men's ward—
the cries of *Alam!* —meaning *pain*—would rise and waver again,
in a ululating howl, ram-jets screaming past the moon,
from the depths of the Baathist beast, the teens, the old men in cabs
riddled with bullets as Baghdad seethed.
Today it began again, and we waited in dread,
knowing no one could ever hope to heal *this*
on our starship of salvation rocketing through the void—
till you, Cassandra Spears, with your Grady-born grace,
deep and wide as Atlanta with its fear-drenched poor,
yelled, Shut up! *I alam!* and as the hubbub eased,
Ya'll make me have alam!—and they laughed through their tears.

Bonded

Loader and gunner, brothers from boot camp days,
they came in one platoon to the shock of the war;
daily they clung together for strength and grace—
each promised to bring the other home once more.
Now both return: two versions of amputee.
It's back to Lejeune, driving with one good hand,
learning how girls are made— will they tend and cleave,
or turn with regret to find an unblemished man?
The road treks hard through rehab, shrinks, the V.A.,
edged nights that dream of friends who couldn't be saved;
the hale will dance and run; few will know what to say,
and pity's worse than hurt to the souls of the brave.

Déjà vu

Back then the look was straight out of Gomer Pyle,
but all I ever knew was hospital blue,
and the rasp, the wince, the ones who vanished at night,
the dread of the dressing cart, its sharps, its tools...
I've been here forty years, and you haven't changed.
You're handsome — God! Your chest! (except for the wounds),
your ribs, your hips — and your look is just the same:
that kicked-dog gaze — Who hurt me? — all confused—

I saw your face the night they started the war,
a necessary pain — they'd thought it through—
and I stayed drunk from weakness, spite, and shame,
because it was all, all, ALL so Déjà vu.

The War Child

You came as a presence there
flung like angel hair
caught in a storm
thrown through a chopper's door
flown with a dozen more
grievously torn.

Limbs turned athletically
dark eyes alight with glee
no sooner laid
down than you left your bed
ran through the ward instead
quite unafraid.

Hearing your grunts and cries
strange how the captive eyes
warmed to the scene
Marines sedated and staid
turned in their nooks and bayed
like Fedayeen.

Oh sing a dance with me
I too am mad you see
grieving and cold
angel of death or dream
tell what our sorrows mean
surely you know.

Drawn by the night's command
load on load of the damned
urged on and on
no one took you away
till you slept, sick of play
close to the dawn.

The Prison Ward

It stands to reason, this howling of many throats,
it fits that this crazed man, his spittle flying,
yells, *You must help him! Help!* amid the din,
shaking his stump at the exit wound in the eye.
He's only been pushed down as far as he can go:
arm off, awful tea, women rampant, no Koran,
nothing's firm anymore— and as a rule,
as all who own a voice can understand,
when everything's lost— you cry.

That wasn't true. There's still a step one level further down,
a place as frozen as that was confused,
the end of many who committed no crime.
Here the wistful, the fretful, with no hate to keep them alive,
who before were dressing, eating, hoping only to be left alone,
settle calmly as wind-swept dust,
hearing, amid the icy silence that now appears,
not even the cry of *Brother!* from ones still with strength to breathe:
the near-defeated howl—but no sound comes
from those blamelessly submitting, as they fold to their knees.

War Nursing
for Cassandra

Another bizarre moment
You clapping
leading
the shattered Iraqi men
around the prison ward
in shambling dance
with a transported
smile on your sweet bronze face
lip-synching your favorite
boom-box music

the Bee Gees' "Stayin' Alive".

Doctor's Amnesia

It can't be rare these days. After the wars,
watching Discovery Channel safe at home,
I saw a form I knew from angled mirrors:
those pinched, frenetic features were my own.
And then the blow of memory's return:
unbearable burns, charred from the waist on down,
scrubbing so fast my fingers seemed to blur,
the flesh, the cries, immediate yet far,
were all as if you viewed them on TV.

I saw the things Prime Time would never see
caught by the cameraman beside the bed.
The child was just the age of my own son.

Ophthalmology

Shot through both eyes, not mercifully dead—
and when the surgeon came in that cold dawn,
I saw with my own eyes the tears his shed
for pity your sight was gone.

Then, in the O.R., grief could only fade
for bodies so bound up in drapes of blue;
how quickly we turned to trifles—sports and the trade
of sewing the sclera through.

Mourning consumes: as much as they cost to make,
even tears may be killed by war, one day.

The Pediatrician's Divorce
for J.B.

The children aren't responsible, they didn't plan to propel
gas against Jerusalem, over others like themselves;
Look at their wounds! you raged, and inwardly asked
if they might hate you because you were a Jew.
And so the light of Israel shone again among the lost.
Dear friend, I saw you then amid the silence of falling ash,
after the rain on Sodom and Gomorrah came down,
not crouched in night but striving like Abraham,
whose unrelenting hands delivered Isaac from his bonds;
and how could she who never saw it understand?

Enemy Wounded

Fedayeen, it's not time for your shot;
Osama would be ashamed.
How foolish of you to want
five minutes without pain!

No. Just bear your wound,
the bright white crown of thorns.
You've faced it all afternoon;
you can tolerate one hour more. *? will he die in an hour?*

Both soldiers!
Both got wounded

28

Soldier

There comes an hour that understands:
The limb that won't ever reach the ground,
The girl who's gone to a different man—
Only the heart's still young and proud.

An hour that flits like a gypsy moth:
The hurtful helpers have done their rounds,
And left an emptiness made of loss—
How to fill it now?

Stopover

Bahrain's hot waist,
narrow as a wasp's,
is nearly closed.

Beyond the Saudi men
seeking drink and girls,
nothing comes or goes.

Bahrain's the mind of the hive
whose towers bleakly hum:
business, business.

Ignoring the muezzin,
the carpet-seller's men
stand you juice and kebab,

but out on the street, the boys
will give you a look or a shove,
meaning: Wait for Iran.

There's a black sun
and a fiery stinger
in Bahrain.

Hospital Visit

Generals don't mind funerals: the dead are simple and shy,
they don't reach out and catch as the wounded do,
and here it isn't a glimpse, a gout, or a single cry:
they've got the whole of the day to corner you.
No wonder the brass runs by with eyes on the clock,
feigning pity, turning grief to a show,
but always some poor soldier's able to shock
them back to the truth they really don't want to know!
General, you writhe now from coming too near—
you're only a fighter because you don't fully see—
come live two weeks on our ward, with the harm we have here—
you'll be mutinous then— and as pacifist as we.

Dressing Change

for Paula

Half Iraq's caked on him,
this bearded Mujahadeen,
and she's the equal of all his strength—
full-breasted, lithe, and clean.

Untouched by bolts of morphine,
his hooded eyes are wild.
Still he sits in the whirlpool,
trusting as any child.

His wounds show fat and fascia:
they gleam like pits of gold.
Water, with weird beauty,
sluices around the holes.

America, overflowing,
Asia of threatened lives,
what a place you choose to meet
under fluorescent skies!

Slick with foam and water,
inward the Q-tips go.
Though he grips and hisses,
  er face never loses its glow.

The Man in the Wound

Quiet the ward, quiet the dressing-cart now,
quiet the morphine drip, blessed easer of pain—
turning his head as I pass, he says, *Hi, Doc,*
asks if I'm working too hard—I look beat—overstrained.
His wound came at Nasiriyah, and I was not there
to shield him from rounds and flame, being safe in the rear;
yet his thought is always of me, the nurse or the friend,
or even the enemy soldier he glimpses or hears.
With arms laid waste, he finds no reason to hate;
his comrades now are all who grieved and withstood:
just as the wound proclaims the hell all have made,
the man in the wound is raised—shown peaceful and good.

Morning on the War Wound Floor

The little monsters are sleeping like the dead,
each in his Holy Friday bed of coals,
etched in the impassivity of those
who carry their doom around in their own heads.
All night you've waited, janglingly awake,
for Jesus' sake who made the mountains move—
at times you thought this hour would never arrive—
success didn't crown you; at least you stayed.
Now, all in a rush, the light that dawns
pours out its furnace down the face of the ward,
leaping the desks, and agitating the beds
like a raider come to release our bonds,

and all the penitents stir, unmesh their eyes,
conjure their stones away, and start to rise.

BATTLE FUGUE

Corpsman

nothing jumps like the medic treasuring the knees
bulked under armorbark landmine distended
needing nie Cross in God's wetted world
indicator of incidence dreamcatcher of loss

carevisions of dross he foreskins into moss
parked in the ass cracks of Amtracs dust grinding
halving the guts over Bob wire hanging
binding up mush moulaged Marine resembling

humps with 3/2 Battalion totallykilledward
shrines out isolated hearts' moment of priest war
scorns the allergy of prime time lectric chaired
jacked up Z Company Fallujah disease

reaches under Kevlar to augur the dawning
flange no wider than fingers torn flesh thin door
flash back to times of homely diarrhea
pack him like you never packed one before

clipping with Kellys abdominal chitlins
pushing trach oncounter Marine boots still on
Sam stick with me Sam you son of a
bitch Sam Squeeze my hand motherfucker Blackhawk into void

cross eyed hopes for a note to hit decision
staunch Red Bull free range overflow opportunity underscored
MREs gulped before MadMinute gets started
Gunny near tears *Doc yore slick's a French whore*

First Blood

In the half shell of the star scattering mind cruisers
Aping the over-ellipsis of an expert hand
He jiggles panicky left right seeking familiar scenes
Urban combat 29 Palms
                              but in discontinuity

Thunder pains them locked to the wall
From street's end to snipers' roof
Gaggles a breathing sun
Cordite taste silver
                    on the
                         starch
                              of the tongue
Knocks chasing hot water rounds rattle the Kevlar sheeting

Hard blows toss tailbones to the ruts of the road *Jesus*
Christ crab scuttle to a dark open door
spitball spouts in the dust of 5000 years'
muddaubed doghating Mesopotamian rage
hopscotch in pursuit of him

Where you at Kirk   Gunny's bored radio voice
Weight stammers flinched impact on thank god brick thick walls
Sit tight we're clearing these fuckers out with grenades

Mindless as the whump whump
Shakes the sleeves of the store

Now sheepish as fire fades
No sweat a few rounds check the pants nothing ribald to show
In the corner old guy crouched eyes wide like he's looking at Mars
with a scared kid underneath him

Engaged

Warrior thrill bow openhanded rampage overflowing
Liquid scenes the proteomic love sticks roar
Carry the red captives to the blue river
Lux code brains mimicking mantras in terse form confusion

Patrols are the same whether termites monkeys or men
Bougainvillead humps already nourishing sweatsoaked vines
Scarce journey to the deeply shadowed part of the isle
Rich tree blood soaking the roots alive with bacteria

The hour of hurt looms large in the beating sun
To make no stop lies limp before the black bull's heel
The very cud of tobacco chaws out Him or me
Violet round into chamber the life-keeping SAW just containable

Pained and rapturous moment when fire is laid
Crashed angels churning the flesh with witless pounding
Hand signals like cops the thrill of a measured run
Bleak in the arms of cover they quake and are free

Danger the main statement of days abandoned to war
The ten per cent tax of the lost stuck fast in the mind-swelling
Wife and children hermetically sealed in the unschooled years
Harsh gift where what they dread most is what you oversee

Love Texted Twice

The magic # of <3 is 12 frm Bagram 2 Rome
Bush dogs n a pck tracking man the biggest giraffe
Brusque dad w/a couple of stripes + 1 or 2 yrs to wield
Ideal fam 100% vote all divergence denied

U can hate a man of the squad tho his black blood's ur own
Not so he who shares sleep n smoke dug hole shits n flies
These couples diverge from Vegas chapels' lore
Rough clone of camo coats <3 beats where ugly is nigh

Terror's the bearable wounding the Doc knits 2 ferry u home
Untenable parting ud hijack a bus 2 get back downrange
Radiant sun of relief as u find them pissing n pure
Thermite night surrounding ull die b4 u let 1 drown

Never such chance of shame in a mil lost ways
The cannibal brunch u brook as a same way ther
The soldier-hearted guilt's the 1 u can't bear alone
None knows but the bro in arms at a place where words expire

Resurrection of raggedy asses looped on the homeward voyage
Gud 2 c wife n kids gr8 knowing that big paw's alive
Clasped trunks on the plane the sweetest armor uve known
Nxt sharing the miracle breath of the flashbcks 2 come

Squad Leader

These soldiers prize nothing but what shoots or wards off steel
Such bulked dinosaurs nearly extinct from the Kevlar mail
Rounds dink hot souls not lakes of cool dominions
Hear O hear He was the Sergeant matchlocked into the lead

They prowled gloomy ghosts down war's tiled jacuzzi
IED and platoon swapped traces till his turned real
Paddywhack bushwhack glommed in the midway dust the

Stryker

rode   its

multicolored   mushroom

thru

its

floor

Smoked view of fate's horizon
     Sprung doors held bleached
          faces longing to seize and flee
Two
     hours clay pigeon
         till the battered shell let go
Ah but the pain came then
    the clamor of breached men's
      keening

By the name the plane swung down
the morphined carpet owned him
Lush on the gantry the flight nurse not
even caring to scout her ass
Landstuhl Balad mere chorus of croakings the frog
pond loosed on vague hoofed minions
munching the homeward path

He learned how wounds
R
eternal
19 surgeries each time the dread corpuscle's
rupture cracked the high thin vault bringing fear withinward
No love could snug the dressing's yank from the carved-out gash

Comes the hour the amputation
just aches to be friendly
Pulled pins' pale pits
let a tired wife's fingers bathe
He wouldn't flock back to Iraq
in a million years
He still can't cosmic he's here
Such gift in each lick
of the life-melon

The V.A. doc gets name job and SSN
No Sir no problem here but what you can see
No rude shock at white cars no piece under the pillow
Just a little less couth with clowns who cope a dent to a deal

Thus the Hard Corps troops who won and lost this war
He'll fix trucks with the same aplomb that watched his death recede
One third killed   one maimed   one blind to the notion of
HURT
His wounds unable to weep till he gives permission to bleed

Safe Home

in the nightmare the seared eyeball's always distended
grown from its socket a lobster's eye goggling
quailed into place with gaze averted gasping
skewed high velocity rounds seeking to nest winking

in the wet brain there is no bar between
moonrise and waking days
and the baby's puke
is a coil of weeping blood
the dreams have rhythm like teams
that make the extra pass
such fear
in finding the mind-soil's

crackt

validation

The pull of danger's an
eerie
dude on the street and
anything (   ) is
a snowflake birthing its blast
you never realized how many
people in (   ) cars there are
caped boogeywhackers looking
4 gaps in the wire

Where trains
of bullet
magnets crawled
nut-to-butt
the burned body found you in a moment-of-someone- else
with a smirk came by and gave him a smoke they
parked a hat
on his head
and turned him
to yourself

In the nightmare random fire
    makes lines in a desert
and you furrow the waste for
water that will not come
    Mother Father
pour me an absolution
the man who clawed the maidens
    is still your son

Fighters

Find all truths out, and these were never alive
Glut-laden how they ghost their war-wrenched mystery's mines
Starting from blank their climb to mercy is manic deeds
They don't mime much, their climacteric's rhymed with tears

Disparity their bent from when they lamed first down
From brute's end to lover's tooth their caged envenomed environs
Show us the man sagged homeward unalive
Our phones have more to learn than learn to count these bricks

Signing plunging ruin to the keeps inside
Hand raptured role in the ranks transformed to vengeful seething
The enemy has clutch where they have lines of brain
Behind them wend the wives where food stamps groom the kids

The Furies' rope unspooled their capped ravines
They hurdled down fate's roof hot-wired past Haji's rooms
Quartered in mournful quartz where they watered machines
Wheeled racks dispatching weakness with rampage and bruise

The Air took metal and made it into a name
Half the cabs in Baghdad riddled beyond repair
Soldiers are not devotees of fracture or stain
They seek the juice of the bud liberality's chair

They are my space allotment from when I was born
I have held their lands in trust as flesh congealed
Many an eye these icy tips have laid to shutness alone
Many a wound these carved grips
have quaking flinched the cockroach of steel

RUINS OF PEACE

The Iraqi Ward

for Mounira

A village always suffers
this one had gowns
old men tea drinkers
there were prayers
and dominoes
and cards though only
half the players had hands

All those were games
you watched but wouldn't play
you were the Muse there
smiling mound
in a black abbayyia
you left your face unveiled
who would hide
such beaming eyes
such rounded cheeks away

Your children dead
within the riddled car
yet you never cried
when we made scarves
you tied them on
the girls who'd lost an arm
you led the prayers
certified the food
and never once broke down

Until the day
the place was disassembled
the healed taken
out to crouching Frogs
for transport home
that was the day you chose
to fall into the arms
of Senior-Chief Minata
the one so good with the kids
a man not your husband
to sway weeping
clasped together
a strange beast
half uniformed half black
crying, Salaam, Salaam!

Nebula

Stolen like a code,
straight within the nail
that breaks through the bone,
wishes are intoned
where no hope avails.

Others are revealed,
silenced overlong.
The Lord's making me
quiver as a reed
suffers in a song.

Darkness grows and grows,
yet the orb of light
that runs like a road,
speaking through the night,
neither ebbs nor flows.

Crossfire

Her scarf blown off, the desert-dwelling bride
evokes a landscape or a constellation,
except no pagan image is portrayed.
Ears, brows, forehead, mouth:

all the lines of a Persian carpet
shine in her now non-living face. A promise
it took the whole warped strength of this wasteland
to erase.

Mantra

warrior bread hot skillet
lamb shank MREs
tea leaves stained water dented
cup shreds of naan

warrior pillow caked mud folded
pack canned meat
Coke bottle stacked wood
numbed hand local dog

warrior hope morning off
flush toilet faces clean
shaven steak short skirts
iced beer padded seat

warrior dream winged round singed
armor plastic sheet
mama san nude spouse
crossed river stranger child

Premonition

To give it credence seems absurd,
and chanting ghosts don't carry guns,
and yet the voice repeats, Third tour.
Third tour is when the ruin comes.

Bad luck to speak a word out loud—
above all else, show self-control,
and keep it from the wife and child
whose eyes turn haggard when you go.

Mountain Burial

for Kristin

Her sealed coffin
lowers into the ground,
far from the gaunt street
where, aiding another,
she caught a mortar round;
as when, back in Balad,
we used to dress her down,
it's just the C.O. and me,
while blank stillness
settles over these
imperturbably green
Pennsylvania hills.

The rifle squad has fired;
the Vets have left their place;
her folks have gone to the wake,
with others yet to soothe,
while mourning the hellion
they struggled to understand.
The parson's words were false:
they praised a simple-hearted
unassuming girl.

Well, so she might have become,
with decades left to grow,
such are the ironies
that mar our briefly known,
imponderable lives;
as through some quirk, even I,
least likely to survive,
am looking down on
the grave of one so young
in my fifty-second year.

We hope so eagerly,
she might have proved a flame
to light a country's way—
incessant, proud, and clean.
We lie to ourselves so well,
she might have lived a tale
we couldn't speak for shame,
have maimed herself, or been
a hundred other women
we'll never love nor learn—

bearing the mysteries—
long ceasing to question why—
knowing we can't retrieve
this well that's now gone dry.
She lives in a field of green
whose thousand blades wave free,
scattered from us by war,
the ender of destinies.

Tradecraft

for Angie Nimmo, R.N.

It wasn't much to you
to walk along these valleys
you knew the knives
the grinding crunch
the sharp intake of air

As long ago one
who blessed and nurtured
forty of these ghosts
(drugging some
dragging some to the morgue
but others
leaning against their girls
walked out with ostomies
metal knees and crutches)

One said to me as he tore
my bandage loose with one
shriek-inducing rip
It's worse if you do it slowly;
you've got to be hard with wounds.

Most of those dead were men
whose lovers forsook them
but now as it all comes again
(and how I hate
to see them shrink from their wounds
cry from pique like children
and gaze at me
with disbelieving eyes
that animal look
that just won't understand)

Through all this you come
pushing your cart
a fragile, gentle woman
and only now do I see
they wave their dressings at you
so that you'll stop
unwind each strip
with infinite care
say, *Sorry, I'm sorry*
every time they wince

Only now do I see
from lines of peace in the face
(which never, never last)
your kind of dressing change
finally proves the best.

There's a world of despair
in tearing
dressings out of a wound.

Happy Return

The war recedes—no killing sounds
nor mounds of flesh that once were friends
(you might be used to it by now)—
until they send you back again.

It's all in place, as if new-born
with undimmed hurt to greet you there;
don't think that time has dulled those thorns—
they're waiting for you— drawing near!

Ship Music

the winding hour comes here
evening fires begin
the thump of the washing machine
feels like an engine's hum

known through steel plates
and who is now at sea
the gliding ship made clean
the red lights dim toward Taps

thin bodies steeped in sleep
packed tight as ropes on racks
compared to a sailor's dream
there is no innocence

Sick Bay unveils a light
a snipe has barked his head
the doctor's roused from bed
irascibility

the Bridge the weeping stars
the course is called then steered
it speaks of older loves
the ones they had when small

trolling the vacant hours
foam patches in the sea
America farewell
the ship is now at sea

Division

Yes, there was newsprint then.
It spoke of sleeves and journeys,
and you could read as far as it went,
the year before the war.

It rained that year,
before the war.
I had my gangly limbs stretched out,
and reached toward the fruit
with awkward, simian hands.
I knew, but cannot remember,
mayflies drowned in syrup,
and brickyards, contrails, stars,
indefensibly young.
Then all turned bronze for a moment,
and every branch that filled the sky
began a slow
vertiginous descent
in particles of ash.

Watchful

While the blizzard passed,
some remained outside,
incompletely seen;
halting hands
limned out the world's
crucifixion and need.

Now the dawn is born:
every roof's a rose,
every street's enflamed.
Heal the lame,
show pity to the poor,
for the good God's reward.

The Eye Surgeon

Coffin after coffin
Seemed to float from the door...   Seamus Heaney, "Casualty"

I

No one shrilled your name,
not with bold stress,
not with looks of pain.
It loomed in treatment rooms
in slurred undertones—
nothing urged on mikes
to charge the P.A.—
barely brought to mind
through the quietest signs—
one of us was gone.

You died suddenly
on a beach far away,
cutting your own throat,
then falling on the blade.
Inexplicable death,
unless, as they said,
surgeries gone bad
drove you to despair—
or maybe some hurt
known only to me,
from lessons we shared
in bays ringed with flame,
there off Iraq
in 2003.

The wounded came conveyed,
helo'd out to board
our high white ship
at anchor near the shore.
You had to cut and sew,
raking off the coals,

ranging through the fire,
and though a lowly flea,
I had steady hands
to hold patiently
flesh as you pursued,
with microscopic care,
sheared iron or bone
through the vitreous fluid,
to save the magic beam—
or, more often, rolled
sclera on globes
of plastic to make
facsimiles of eyes.
The time we had to treat
that friendly Iraqi man
who'd mobbed the U.S. troops,
who then shot through his face
for seeming to mean harm,
I watched you weep yourself
with tears he couldn't see
while telling him he was blind.

You told a tale that night
dating from Vietnam—
another hospital ship,
during your corpsman phase:
the Ophtho Doc was found
drunk on purloined booze,
unthinkably impaired
(though luckily he had
no fresh wounds to mind),
at which point he claimed
in thick disgusting tones,
it was his birthday then,
and that day he'd done
a milestone of the cruise:
his hundredth enucleation.
Mired in disgrace,
inept and feeling wronged,

he had to sleep it off,
and back then you thought
he simply wasn't strong.

As one who didn't drink,
you hid your anger well.
I didn't see it again
until the homeward voyage,
when, moored in Italy,
we staged the poor in lines
halfway around the quay
to have glasses made,
and you, the Ophtho head
cancelled all liberty,
and worked us 48 hours,
while others toured and played,
till all of them could see.

II

I keep thinking back
to days before the war,
on Circe's isle,
or was it Baltic shores:
you and I fought
over a jeweled charm,
white amber in gold,
the choicest in the store—
I'd laid it down on hold,
you claimed it for your own,
and how we yelled and swore
there in full uniform,
scaring all the staff,
till I gave it up
as an unlucky stone.
Having read your moods,
your rage when deemed wrong,
your fury at the thought
right could be denied,

I wish I'd seen you once
the night you chose to die,
because I would've known.

Midnight strikes as clear
as those we chimed at sea,
drawing hard stars
that blink across the sky.
The pint of wine I've drunk
for sleep, burns emptily.
Steve, the war goes on,
with unrelenting blasts,
as when the desert flings
sandstorms over the land.
I'm told with time you'll be
tranquil in memory,
a smiling peaceful man.
Stay yourself toward me.
Turn that look of yours,
your stiff resisting brow,
on those you left behind.
Friend passed to the waves
in military style,
my hundredth eye gone blind,
I'm burying you now.

Rock Creek PTSD

Rock Creek tumbles as
daylight ends, its water pours
over straits and bends,
flinging its way through
spouts and flumes,
as human
fortune collides with doom.

Tumult issued in
roaring sounds
clears the mist as
the rush tilts down
to freezing deeps and
pernicious bogs,
bleakly featured with fallen logs.

You soothed my suffering mind before,
and how I wish
you were not transformed,
turned so fatal
in each detail,
your clean bright energy leached
and paled.

I shun, like
fever's ferocities,
such haunted boulders and
frightened trees,
all over the creek an expanse
of foam,
quick jets
like blood, flung
chips like bone.

You chimed your wish in Fallujah's ear,
and twilight echoed
as it does here;
how many heroes
in those harsh days
fell into your flood
and were borne away!

Rock Creek, measure of all my fears,
I curse your crying with my own tears:
fury sweeping
across this ground,
return my brothers
whom you have drowned!

After Three Years

Sergeant Soarez was impossible to kill
his squad took RPG's from the Fedayeen
they were pinned down and hurting when the life-giving A-10's came in
strafed the wrong way and (excuse me) shot off his ass

he came through our triage on that frenzied night
the first day at Nasiriyah the war shrieked like the mad
Soarez in Bay 4 I thought would never walk again
he was nothing but meatloaf from the back to the thighs

23 surgeries later he tried to stay Marines but couldn't wall-climb
now he's leaving to work with groups that won't abide war
as soon as I read Soarez it was a movie I knew by heart
I saw him and the others, cored Rice and Hurst with torn bowels

You bet I recognized Soarez today in the waiting room
though his face was contorted the last time we met
I reeled off the dictation, I didn't need the chart
I knew my old friend, knew each inch of his poor ass

Uncle Jim

You wanted to die amid your Marines.
That thought was a law you made into a life;
knowing the cold of Chosin, you came to harbor here,
growing more father and friend to the final day.

In answer to destruction, your call was toward bricks:
the Spartan boy with the fox was the favorite tale you knew.
You drew me from selfishness to fruitful work,
and so I became a steward to men of arms.

Now that you're gone, there will be no one else
to carry the weight of life, a weight you made lighter for me.
I'll pick up your death like a mortar base plate,
as troops do when the stronger man goes down,

for those around you are uncomplaining still—
with shattered trunks and limbs, they ask if they've done well.
The air stands high over quiet Bethesda now,
as one more general joins his bright Marines.

They say everything's been written; it hasn't.
Darkness and light are vast, and poets have barely begun.
Even when it hides, the hand knows when it's writing a final death.
Like the heart's, its mourning is always new.

Blood Brothers

The fight swirled down from the roof
where the troops went in,
and somehow, amid confusion
and acrid haze,
these two fell down
together: a beardless Marine
poured out on a Mujahadeen
killed by grenades.

The air still rings
that this is what we
give to attain our ends;
but where their comrades grieve,
on sandaled feet
or armored knees,
their lying thus, beneath
the vows of those who
guide but don't draw aim,
renders them clear
in ways the fire creators can't conceive:

Not dead for freedom— love will build that another way;
not dead for faith— denier of all misdeeds.
The evil is never the necessary:
each one killed is a ruin of peace.

Wife on the ICU

I watch at night and walk at dawn
forever in flight like the soul of a bird
the monitor shows a thin green line
I walk at night and watch at dawn
not knowing the end of the road I'm on
down which, possessed by a voice unheard
I watch at night and walk at dawn
forever in flight like the soul of a bird

Intensive Care

Two left boots
presaged
a broken text.
They stood alone
between a phone
and a hard grey floor.
One hour passed
and tremors lapsed
down like veins of honey
speech grew slack
and on your back
a lake of fire
quivered and poured.
> *How long does fever take?*
> *Who pulls the brake*
> *on limbs that used to*
> *charge and dance?*

Dreams were bright cotillions
shedding fruit
like pennies down a chute
where trees of wax
explored the not-quite-underground.
Green pots of pain
flowered and then
went out again.
Never such
exhausted loss of touch
as when you tapped
Escape Escape
across a painted board.
> *A yapping pack*
> *explores your lack*
> *of previous*
> *exactitude.*

More than sex
is syncopated
needing frames
to make you stand at ease.
Need means lack
burning through a coal black
haze
in spots of rays
that trap you like the Book
while fears uncoil
thick as pools of oil
in storms without sound.

The strangest
sun that rose
came through holes
in the day's
rank order.
Yesterday
we ate your cake in different ways
I back grown sore
from having hope destruct once more
beat them to their knees
with bitter prophesies.
Your mother cried
your sister muttered
words I couldn't understand
toward your husband
sitting like a ship.
　　He runs his hand
　　across his wedding band
　　as if to change
　　its shape.

Tomb of the Unknown

The sentry paces in gold and blue,
At measure the morning long—
As fine a face as you ever knew,
Self-mastered, rapt, and strong.

But where they bury beyond the hill,
Fresh graves despoil the green,
In testimony to what he wills
And what his virtues mean.

I dream of an army that bears no shame—
Original grace restored—
War-courage without the killed and lamed,
A soldier without a sword.

Third View of the Dis-enhearted

Christmas
on the Neuro ward.
Not a sigh
except the ventilators.
If my pulse
only would go down,
I'd sleep awhile.
I've devolved,
like a mist
on growing plots of snow,
and all my thoughts ring tired:
faded tracks
of caribou
tumbled into words—

> *this is the holy night*
> *the holy year*
> *with strains of resurrection*
> *lyrical and clear*
> *to listen is to hold*
> *the night within*
> *to venture in*
> *these bodies' still repose*

Slipping
through a chain of places,
I commanded
those who held my halters.
Strange to be
stripped of every room
the royal state requires,
while like an urge,
my bowels and breathing
slither through your hands—
how could I dream
the ten per cent
chance of some miscarriage
meant it could be mine—

look back on malls of gold
on highway gloom
on lines of homes like ranks
of multicolored tombs
is this deliverance
or further loss
or just one more
face within the nail

Through the gleam
of scattered greens and purples,
people range.
Surgeons rub their glasses
with a sigh:
large carts edge by,
while nurses glow
in flowing scrubs that open
where they bend.
Deny all wives
the right to enter in:
this beauty's broad
nipples are
too bold for such display—

oh banks of blonde seducers
standing by
to bed one crucifixion
virginal and shy
in hopes the issue of that
love might be
a mystery
enough to turn
the angel from the door

Floated
in between the lines
of overriding snow,
eloquence subsides.
You drag a moistened
swab across my lips,
in bays so coyly labeled
Donder's room
and Blitzen's room,
while Christian anthems
(do you hear what I hear)
make the silence
undeniably real—

> *And we turn back to ask*
> *each listener*
> *whether fear can ever*
> *turn beautiful*
> *whether there's really*
> *someone watching you*
> *holding you*
> *faithfully*
> *and wishing away your pain*
> *through interdigitated*
> *light*

I'm with you till the night
gives up
its name.

CODA

The Gunner, John

Pity him here, his skull crushed by a tread—
beneath the mud pressed out, one intact jaw,
some teeth at ninety degrees, the scraps of a tongue—
Was he no more than *this*? No, this was a mask;
place it in calm beneath the ground,
and when he takes it off he'll still be whole.

NOTES

The Hurt Fedayeen: A Fedayeen is an irregular Muslim fighter. "Fedayeen" refers to a generic fighter; "Mujahadeen" to one fighting for a religious cause (such as expulsion of U.S. forces from Muslim lands).

Nursing the Iraqis: DoD stands for U.S. Department of Defense.

Soldiers' Chorus: An AK is an AK-47 assault rifle (insurgent weapon), an RPG is a Rocket-Propelled Grenade (insurgent weapon), and a TOW is a U.S. antitank rocket.

Night Mission: Frog is slang for a CH-46 troop-carrying helicopter.

Ahmed the Soldier: F.A.E. stands for Fuel-Air Explosive.

Space Travel: Grady is the public hospital of Atlanta.

Déjà vu: In 1967, I was a patient on a ward of Marine wounded from Vietnam. Gomer Pyle was an amiable Marine in a TV sitcom.

The War Child: During the Iraq war, some villagers tossed unwanted children (often ones with cognitive disabilities) onto American helicopter MEDEVACs in order to get rid of them.

Doctor's Amnesia: This poem relates the memory of a patient whose case I repressed until I saw myself treating him in a TV documentary about the ship.

Corpsman: From the lexicon of battlefield medicine:
  Amtrac: a Marine fighting vehicle
  Moulage: wound mockup used in training
  Kelly: a surgical clamp
  Trach: tracheotomy: cutting open the windpipe to ease breathing
  MRE: constipating "Meals Ready to Eat" battle ration (also called "Meals Resistant to Excretion")
  MadMinute: traditional infantry tactic of mass blind firing to disclose a hidden enemy
  Gunny: Marine Gunnery Sergeant

First Blood: 29 Palms refers to a Marine desert training base.

Engaged: SAW: Squad Automatic Weapon

Squad Leader: A Stryker is an Army fighting vehicle.

Fighters: Haji is slang for a Muslim soldier. "Cockroach of steel" refers to metal in the wound. Thanks to Wilfred Owen and Walt Whitman for beginning and end lines.

The Iraqi Ward: An abbiyyia is a women's garment that cloaks the entire body, worn by many Iraqi women and others who follow certain Islamic traditions. Frogs are helicopters.

Mantra: Naan is a round flatbead that commonly accompanies a hot meal in West Asian and Middle Eastern countries.

Mountain Burial: C.O. stands for Commanding Officer.

Tradecraft: Tradecraft is an intelligence officer's term for studied expertise.

Ship Music: A snipe is an engineering department sailor.

The Eye Surgeon: A flea is a nonsurgical physician. Enucleation refers to the surgical removal of the eye.

Rock Creek PTSD: PTSD stands for post-traumatic stress disorder. Walter Reed Army Medical Center was located near Rock Creek Park in Washington, D.C.

After Three Years: An A-10 is a ground-support aircraft.

Uncle Jim: Chosin refers to the Chosin Reservoir, an important battle in the Korean War. Bethesda indicates Bethesda Naval Hospital.

Intensive Care: "The Book" refers to military regulations.

ABOUT THE AUTHOR

Frederick Foote is a retired U.S. Navy physician who lives in Bethesda, Maryland. His work has appeared in *Commonweal, JAMA, The Progressive,* and many other journals. He is the director of the Warrior Poetry Project at Walter Reed National Military Medical Center. To learn more about this book, the author, and his upcoming appearances, visit **www.medicagainstbomb.com**.

ACKNOWLEDGEMENTS

Grateful acknowledgement is made to the following publications where these poems first appeared:

Antietam Review: "Morning on the War Wound Floor"

Blue Collar Review: "Hospital Visit"

Commonweal: A Review of Religion, Politics, and Culture: "The Gunner, John"

Gargoyle: "Space Travel" and "Division"

Haight Ashbury Literary Journal: "Soldier"

The Journal of the American Medical Association (JAMA): "Bonded," "Doctor's Amnesia," "The Iraqi Ward," "Local News," and "The Man in the Wound"

The Little Patuxent Review: "First Blood" and "Night Mission"

Mediphors: "Wife on the ICU"

The Meridian Anthology of Contemporary Poetry: "Third View of the Dis-enhearted"

Pegasus Review: "Nebula"

The Progressive: "Nursing the Iraqis," "You Gave the Iraqis Their Scarves," and "War Nursing"

The South Carolina Review: "The Hurt Fedayeen"

Southern I: "Déjà vu"

Special thanks to those who helped me complete and revise this manuscript:

Ginny Connors of Grayson Books, Editor Extraordinaire

Anne-Marie Blum ("the Mother of all teachers") and Ed Perlman of the John Hopkins M.A. in Writing Program

Nancy Naomi Carlson ("the Fountain of all improvements")

Areej Nitowski who reviewed my pidgin Arabic

Fellow Vet writers who reviewed for military accuracy: Ron Capps, Richard Lowry, Jim Matthews, Janis Albuquerque, Mike Fay and Dick Epstein

This book is our gift.